TABLE OF CONTENTS

THE SOUL'S DELIGHT

Selected Writings of
EVELYN UNDERHILL

Upper Room Spiritual Classics — Series 2

Selected, edited, and introduced by
Keith Beasley-Topliffe

UPPER
ROOM BOOKS

Art direction: Michele Wetherbee
Interior design and layout: Nancy Cole

First Printing: October 1998

Library of Congress Cataloging-in-Publication Data

Underhill, Evelyn, 1875–1941.
    The soul's delight: selected writings of Evelyn Underhill.
        p.   cm. — (Upper Room spiritual classics. Series 2)
    ISBN 0-8358-0837-8
    1. Mysticism. 2. Spiritual life—Anglican Communion. I.
Title. II. Series.
BV5095.U5A25   1998
248.2'2—dc21   97-13414
                                                                    CIP

Printed in the United States of America

INTRODUCTION

Homely seems a strange word to apply to the spiritual life. But for Evelyn Underhill, it captured the essence of mysticism as a humble, practical, simple, everyday way of relating to God. She was sure that all could learn to be mystics, to have a deep, personal experience of God's love at work in their own lives. In her scholarly works, she described the life of prayer and worship and introduced modern readers to many spiritual classics. As a retreat leader and radio speaker, she offered plain advice for spotting and removing the blocks in the spiritual life, for opening oneself to God.

Underhill stood strongly for the basics of the Christian life against the fads of her day. At a time when psychologists were proclaiming that religion was an illusion, she insisted that it was grounding oneself in the Ultimate Reality. At a time when Christian leaders were proclaiming the centrality of social outreach, she insisted that fellowship and service were not the essence of Christianity, but only the symptoms of a life grounded in adoration of God. She knew that only a life filled with God's love could have the tranquillity, gentleness, and strength to keep offering that love to others in a world filled with hatred and violence.

EVELYN UNDERHILL'S WORLD

When Evelyn Underhill was born in 1875, Queen Victoria reigned over a British Empire that circled the globe. That state of affairs continued pretty much unchanged for the first quarter century of her life, until Victoria's death in 1901. England was the most powerful nation in what seemed to be a world of steady intellectual and moral progress. The world was becoming civilized and Christianized, even in remote areas. Peace and prosperity could continue forever, it seemed.

That dream ended with World War I (1914–18), followed by the Communist revolution in Russia and the rise of fascism in Spain and Italy and Nazism in Germany. By Underhill's death in 1941, with London under regular bombing, the world seemed a much grimmer place.

The same period saw a great scientific and technological revolution. A series of inventions—telephone (1876), electric light (1879), radio (1895), and motion pictures (1895)—transformed the worlds of communication and entertainment. Automobiles (ca. 1890) and airplanes (1903) changed both transportation and warfare. Such examples of the triumph of science led to a desire for similar scientific approaches to the human mind and spirit.

In 1890, William James, an American psychologist and philosopher, published *The Principles of Psychology*. A few years later Sigmund Freud, an Austrian doctor, began to publish descriptions of psychoanalysis. Both men turned their attention to religion. In *The Varieties of Religious Experience* (1902), James examined conversion and peak experiences. Freud attacked religion as an illusion in several early works and more thoroughly in *The Future of an Illusion* (1927). Such works served as a background for (or counterpoint to) Underhill's attempts at an objective analysis of mysticism.

Evelyn Underhill's Life

Evelyn Underhill was born on December 6, 1875, in Wolverhampton, England. Her father was a lawyer and yachting enthusiast. Her youth was fairly typical for a Victorian-era girl, with education in boarding school and at King's College, London. Although she was baptized as an infant in the Church of England, she took little interest in that church as a young adult. She became interested in religious experience in general in the early 1900s. She dabbled in the occult as part of a group called the Golden Dawn, visited convents, and most important, read extensively. By about 1907, she considered herself a Christian and seriously pondered becoming a Roman Catholic. She held back, partly in deference to the wishes of her new husband, Hubert Stuart Moore (a lawyer whom she had married after seventeen years of courtship), and partly in response to Catholic attacks on modernism and biblical study.

Her first major publications were short stories, novels, and books of poetry. Then, in 1911, she published *Mysticism: A Study of the Nature and Development of Man's Spiritual Consciousness*. In it she combined a thorough historical study with a theoretical description of individual spiritual growth. It was followed by many other books, both translations of spiritual classics and other books on mysticism, including *The Mystical Way* (1912), *Practical Mysticism* (1914), and *The Essentials of Mysticism* (1920). During World War I, Evelyn Underhill did charity work among the wives and widows of soldiers and sailors and also prepared or translated travel guides for Naval Intelligence. Her husband took time from his law practice to design and make artificial limbs.

Three major changes took place in 1921–22. Evelyn Underhill embraced the Church of England and began to worship regularly. She was invited to give a series of lectures (published as *The Life of the Spirit and the Life of Today*) at Manchester College, Oxford—the first woman to receive such an invitation. And she began to receive spiritual direction from Baron Friedrich von Hügel, a Roman Catholic theologian who lived in England. He continued to meet and correspond with her until his death in 1925.

Underhill's life became more and more taken up with writing (including many book reviews and introductions to books by others), leading retreats, and giving individual spiritual direction to others. In 1936, she published *Worship*, a scholarly study of the theology, history, and practice of Christian worship, which soon became a standard introduction to the subject. Although she had written in defense of just war during World War I, she became convinced that true Christianity demanded pacifism, and she urged prayer and action for peace as World War II began. Her own activities were greatly cut back by increasing problems with asthma. She died at home in London on June 15, 1941.

FURTHER READING

Many of Evelyn Underhill's books are still in print, including *Mysticism*, *The Spiritual Life*, and *Worship*. *Practical Mysticism* is a good, readable introduction to her early thought. Many of her retreat talks were published, including some recently found and printed in *The Ways of the Spirit*, as well as those used in the selections here. Clergy might especially want to read *Concerning the Inner Life*.

There are several biographies, including *Evelyn Underhill: An Introduction to Her Life and Writings* by Christopher Armstrong, which has been of great help in preparing this introduction, and more recently *Evelyn Underhill: Artist of the Infinite Life* by Dana Greene.

Underhill read so widely that it would be hard to single out important influences. She frequently refers to the *Confessions* of Augustine, *The Cloud of Unknowing*, *The Imitation of Christ*, and the works of the Carmelites Teresa of Avila, John of the Cross, and Brother Lawrence. Of von Hügel's works, she recommends *Letters to a Niece* and *Life of Prayer*.

NOTE ON THE TEXT

The selections here are taken from published retreats, radio talks, and letters and so have a more relaxed and "homely" style than her more formal and scholarly works. They have been edited for length and inclusive language. Punctuation, spelling, and grammar have been Americanized, as have some words and idioms. Scripture quotations and allusions have been conformed to the New Revised Standard Version where possible.

# PRACTICAL SPIRITUALITY

From *The Spiritual Life*, Part 1

In 1936, Underhill gave a series of four radio talks intended to present the basics of the Christian's spiritual life in simple language. They were later expanded for publication as The Spiritual Life. *This selection from the first talk addresses Underhill's central theme, the practicality of a life anchored in God.*

Indeed, if God is All and God's Word to us is All, that must mean that God is the reality and controlling factor of every situation, religious or secular; and that it is only for God's glory and creative purpose that it exists. Therefore our favorite distinction between the spiritual life and the practical life is false. We cannot divide them. One affects the other all the time: for we are creatures of sense and of spirit, and must live an amphibious life. Christ's whole Ministry was an exhibition, first in one way and then in another, of this mysterious truth. It is through all the circumstances of existence, inward and outward, not only those we like to label spiritual, that we are pressed to our right position and given our supernatural food. For a spiritual life is simply a life in which all that we do comes from the center, where we are anchored in God: a life soaked through and through by a sense of God's reality and claim, and self-given to the great movement of God's will.

Most of our conflicts and difficulties come from trying to deal with the spiritual and practical aspects of our life separately instead of realizing them as parts of one whole. If our practical life is centered on our own interests; cluttered up by possessions; distracted by ambitions, passions, wants, and worries; beset by a sense of our own rights and importance, or anxieties for our own future, or longings for our own success; we need not expect that our spiritual life will be a contrast to all this. The soul's house is not built on such a convenient plan: there are few soundproof partitions in it. Only when the conviction—not merely the idea—that the demand of the Spirit, however inconvenient, comes first and *is* first, rules the whole of it, will those objectionable noises die down that have a way of penetrating into the nicely furnished little oratory, and drowning all the quieter voices by their din.

Saint John of the Cross, in a famous and beautiful poem, described the beginning of the journey of his soul to God:

> One dark night,
> Fired with love's urgent longings
> —Ah, the sheer grace!—
> I went out unseen,
> My house being now all stilled.

Not many of us could say that. Yet there is no real occasion for tumult, strain, conflict, anxiety, once we have reached the living conviction that God is All. All takes place within God. God alone matters; God alone is. Our spiritual life is God's affair, because whatever we may think to the contrary, it is really produced by God's steady attraction and our humble and self-forgetful response to it. It consists in being drawn, at God's pace and in God's way, to the place where God wants us to be, not the place we fancied for ourselves.

Some people may seem to us to go to God by a moving staircase; where they can assist matters a bit by their own efforts, but much gets done for them and progress does not cease. Some appear to be whisked past us in an elevator, while we find ourselves on a steep flight of stairs with a bend at the top so that we cannot see how much farther we have to go. But none of this really matters. What matters is the conviction that all are moving toward God, and in that journey, accompanied, supported, checked, and fed by God. Since our dependence on God is absolute, and our desire is that God's Will shall be done, this great desire can gradually swallow up, neutralize all our small, self-centered desires. When that happens life, inner and outer, becomes one single, various act of adoration and self-giving; one undivided response of the creature to the demand and pressure of Creative Love.

 # тbe bеакт оf тbе
Lifе оf ркаyек

From *Concerning the Inner Life*, Chapter 2

Concerning the Inner Life *grew out of a retreat for
parish clergy and was published in 1926. Here Underhill
talks about adoration as the heart and starting point for all
prayer.*

Take first then, as primary, the achievement
and maintenance of a right attitude toward God; that
profound and awestruck sense of God's transcendent
reality, that humbly adoring relation, on which all
else depends. I feel no doubt that, for all who take
the spiritual life seriously, this prayer of adoration
exceeds all other types in educational and purifying
power. It alone is able to consolidate our sense of the
supernatural, to conquer our persistent self-occupation, to expand our spirits, to feed and quicken our
awareness of the wonder and the delightfulness of
God. There are two movements that must be plainly
present in every complete spiritual life. The energy of
its prayer must be directed on the one hand towards
God; and on the other toward people. The first
movement embraces the whole range of spiritual
communion between the soul and God; in it we turn
toward Divine Reality in adoration, bathing, so to
speak, our souls in the Eternal Light. In the second
we return, with the added peace and energy thus
gained, to the natural world; there to do spiritual

work for and with God for others. Thus prayer, like the whole of our inner life, "swings between the unseen and the seen." Now both these movements are of course necessary in all Christians; but the point is that the second will only be well done where the first has the central place. The deepening of the soul's unseen attachments must precede the outward swing toward the world in order to safeguard it.

This means that adoration, and not intercession or petition, must be the very heart of the life of prayer. For prayer is a supernatural activity or nothing at all; and it must primarily be directed to supernatural ends. It, too, acknowledges the soul's basic law: It comes from God, belongs to God, is destined for God. It must begin, end, and be enclosed in the atmosphere of adoration, aiming at God for and in God's self. Our ultimate effect as transmitters of heavenly light and love directly depends on this adoring attentiveness. In such a prayer of adoring attentiveness, we open our doors wide to receive God's ever-present Spirit; abasing ourselves and acknowledging our own nothingness. Only the soul that has thus given itself to God becomes part of the mystical body through which God acts on life. Its destiny is to be the receiver and transmitter of grace.

Is not that practical work? For Christians, surely, the only practical work. But sometimes we are in such a hurry to transmit that we forget our primary duty is to receive; and that God's self-imparting through us, will be in direct proportion to our adoring love and humble receptiveness. Only when our souls are filled to the brim, can we presume to offer spiritual gifts to others. The remedy for that sense of impotence, that desperate spiritual exhaustion that religious workers too often know, is, I am sure, an inner life governed not by petition but by adoring prayer. When we find that the demands made upon us are seriously threatening our inward poise, when we feel symptoms of starvation and stress, we can be quite sure that it is time to call a halt, to reestablish the fundamental relation of our souls with Eternal Reality, the Home and Father of our spirits. "Our hearts shall have no rest except in you." It is only when our hearts are thus actually at rest in God, in peaceful and self-oblivious adoration, that we can hope to show God's attractiveness to others.

In the flood tide of such adoring prayer, the soul is released from the strife and confusions of temporal life; it is lifted far beyond all petty controversies, petty worries, and petty vanities-and none of us escape these things. It is carried into God, hidden in God. This is the only way in which it can achieve the utter self-forgetfulness that is the basis of its peace and power and that can never be ours as long as we make our prayer primarily a means of drawing gifts to ourselves and others from God, instead of an act of unmeasured self-giving. I am certain that we gradually and imperceptibly learn more about God by this persistent attitude of humble adoration than we can hope to do by any amount of mental exploration. For in it our soul recaptures, if only for a moment, the fundamental relation of the tiny created spirit with its Eternal Source; and the time is well spent that is spent in getting this relation and keeping it right. In it we breathe deeply the atmosphere of Eternity; and when we do that, humility and common sense are found to be the same thing. We realize, and rerealize, our tininess, our nothingness, and the greatness and steadfastness of God. And we all know how priceless such a realization is for those who have to face the grave spiritual risk of presuming to teach others about God.

Moreover, from this adoring prayer and the joyous self-immolation that goes with it, all the other prayerful dispositions of our souls seem ultimately to spring. A deep, humble contrition, a sense of our creaturely imperfection and unworthiness, gratitude for all that is given us, burning and increasing charity that longs to spend itself on other souls-all these things are signs of spiritual vitality. And spiritual vitality depends on the loving adherence of our spirits to God. Thus it is surely of the first importance for those who are called to exacting lives of service to determine that nothing shall interfere with the development and steady, daily practice of loving and adoring prayer, a prayer full of intimacy and awe. It alone maintains the soul's energy and peace, and checks the temptation to leave God for God's service. I think that if you have only as little as half an hour to give each morning to your private prayer,

it is not too much to make up your minds to spend
half that time in such adoration. For it is the central
service asked by God of human souls; and its neglect
is responsible for much lack of spiritual depth and
power. Moreover, it is more deeply refreshing,
pacifying, and assuring than any other type of
prayer. But only those know this who are practiced
in adoring love.

 ADORATION

From *The Spiritual Life*, Part 2

This selection continues the theme of adoration, central to Underhill's understanding of prayer. Cardinal Pierre de Bérulle (1575-1629), was a French priest and diplomat and the author of several books on prayer.

One of the great French teachers of the seventeenth century, Cardinal de Bérulle, summed up our relation to God in three words: Adoration, Adherence, Cooperation. This means that from first to last the emphasis is to be on God and not on ourselves. Admiring delight, not begging demands. Faithful and childlike dependence—a clinging to the Invisible, as the most real of all realities, in all the vicissitudes of life—not mere self-expression and self-fulfillment. Disinterested collaboration in the Whole, in God's vast plan and purpose; not concentration on our own small affairs. Three kinds of generosity. Three kinds of self-forgetfulness. There we have the formula of the spiritual life: a confident reliance on the immense fact of God's Presence, everywhere and at all times, pressing on the soul and the world by all sorts of paths and in all sorts of ways, pouring out on it God's undivided love, and demanding an undivided loyalty. The discovery that this is happening all the time, to the just and the unjust—and that we are simply being invited to adore and to serve what is already there—

once it has become a living conviction for us, will inevitably give to our spiritual life a special quality of gratitude, realism, trust. We stand in a world completely penetrated by the Living God, the abiding Source and Sum of Reality. We are citizens of that world now; our whole life is or should be an acknowledgment of this.

> If I ascend to heaven, you are there;
> if I make my bed in Sheol, you are there.
> If I take the wings of the morning
> and settle at the farthest limits of the sea,
> even there your hand shall lead me,
> and your right hand shall hold me fast

Consider for a moment what, in practice, the word adoration implies. The upward and outward look of humble and joyful admiration. Awestruck delight in the splendor and beauty of God, the action of God and Being of God, in and for God's self alone, as the very color of life: giving its quality of unearthly beauty to the harshest, most disconcerting forms and the dreariest stretches of experience. This is adoration: not a difficult religious exercise, but an attitude of the soul. "To you I lift up my eyes, O you who are enthroned in the heavens!" I don't turn around and look at myself. Adoration begins to purify us from egotism straight away. It may not always be easy-in fact, for many people it is not at all easy-but it is realism; the atmosphere within which alone the spiritual life can be lived. *Our Father in heaven, hallowed be your Name!* That tremendous declaration, with its unlimited confidence and unlimited awe, governs everything else.

What a contrast this almost inarticulate act of measureless adoration is to what Karl Barth calls the dreadful prattle of theology. *Hallowed be your Name*: not described or analyzed be your Name. Before that Name, let the most soaring intellects cover their eyes with their wings, and adore. Compared with this, even the coming of the Kingdom and the doing of the Will are side issues; particular demonstrations of the Majesty of the Infinite God, on whom all centers, and for whom all is done. People who are apt to say that adoration is difficult, and it is so much easier to pray for practical things, might remember that in making this great act of adoration they are praying for extremely practical things: among others, that their own characters, homes, social contacts, work, conversation, amusements, and politics may be cleansed from imperfection, sanctified. For all these are part of God's Universe. God's Name must be hallowed in and through them if they are to be woven into the Divine world and made what they were meant to be.

A spiritual life involves the setting of our will toward all this. The Kingdom must come as a concrete reality, with a power that leaves no dark corners outside its radius; and the Will be done in this imperfect world, as it is in the perfect world of

Eternity. What really seems to you to matter most? The perfection of God's mighty symphony, or your own remarkably clever performance of that difficult passage for the tenth violin? And again, if the music unexpectedly requires your entire silence, which takes priority in your feelings? The mystery and beauty of God's orchestration? Or the snub administered to you? Adoration, widening our horizons, drowning our limited interests in the total interests of Reality, redeems the spiritual life from all religious pettiness and gives it a wonderful richness, meaning, and span. And more, every aspect, even the most homely, of our practical life can become part of this adoring response, this total life; so it always has done in those who have achieved full spiritual personality. "All the earth worships you" means what it says. The life, beauty, and meaning of the whole created order, from the tomtit to the Milky Way, refers back to the Absolute Life and Beauty of its Creator: and so perceived, so lived, every bit has spiritual significance. Thus the old woman of the legend could boil her potatoes to the greater glory of God; and Saint Teresa, taking her turn in the kitchen, found God very easily among the pots and pans.

hallowing the Name

From *Abba*, Chapter 3

Abba is another collection of retreat addresses, this time based on the Lord's Prayer. The retreat was held in 1934, but the book was not published until 1940. Here Underhill explains how we hallow God's name, not only with our adoration but also with our whole lives. The quote from Martin Buber (1878–1965), a Jewish philosopher and theologian, is taken from his most famous book, I and Thou.

This first response of creation to its author, this awestruck hallowing of the Name, must also be the first response of the praying soul. If we ask how this shall be done within the individual life and what it will require of us in oblation and adjustment, perhaps the answer will be something like this: "*Our Father in heaven, hallowed,* revered, *be your* mysterious *Name* in my dim and fluctuating soul, to which you have revealed yourself in such a degree as I can endure. May all my contacts and relationships, my struggles and temptations, thoughts, dreams, and desires be colored by this loving reverence. Let me ever look through and beyond circumstance to you, so that all I am and do may become more and more worthy of the God who is the origin of all. Let me never take such words on my lips that I could not pass from them to the hallowing of your Name. (That one principle alone, consistently applied, would bring order and charity into the center of my life.) May that Name, too, be hallowed in my work, keeping me in remembrance that you are the doer of all that is really done; my part is that of a humble collaborator, giving of my best." This means that adoration, a delighted recognition of the life and action of God, subordinating everything to the Presence of the Holy, is the essential preparation for action. That stops all feverish strain, all rebellion and despondency, all sense of our own importance, all worry about our own success and so gives dignity, detachment, tranquillity to our action and may make it of some use to God.

Thus the four words of this petition can cover, criticize, and reinterpret the whole of our personal life; cleansing it from egoism, orienting it toward reality, and reminding us that our life and work are without significance except insofar as they glorify that God to whom nothing is adequate though everything is dear. Our response to each experience God puts in our path, from the greatest disclosure of beauty to the smallest appeal to love, from perfect happiness to utmost grief, will either hallow or not hallow God's Name; and this is the only thing that matters about it. For every call to admiration or to sacrifice is an intimation of the Holy, the Other; it opens a path leading out from self to God. These words, then, form in themselves a complete prayer, an aspiration that includes every level and aspect of life. It is the sort of prayer that both feeds and expresses the life of a saint, in its absolute disinterestedness and delighted abasement before the Perfection of God.

From one point of view the rest of the Lord's Prayer is simply about the different ways in which this adoring response of creation can be made more complete for it asks for the sanctification of the universe. And by universe we do not mean some vast abstraction. We mean everything that exists: visible and invisible, the small as well as the great, the hosts of earth as well as the hosts of heaven, the mouse's tail as well as the seraph's wing brought into the circle of holiness and transfigured by the radiance of God. All creatures without exception taking part in the one great utterance of the Name: all selfinterested striving transformed into that one great striving for the Glory of God that is the whole life of heaven and should be the whole life of earth.

"If," says Martin Buber, "you explore the life of things and of conditioned being you come to the unfathomable, if you deny the life of things and of conditioned being, you stand before nothingness, if you hallow this life you meet the living God." Here is declared the principle of cosmic order that must govern the coming of the Kingdom and doing of the Will and shall at its term convert the whole world of action into an act of worship. Since this world of action includes the small but powerful movements of the individual soul, here, too, the law of the Cosmos is to be applied. For this soul's life, if indeed that soul is truly living, must be that of a spirit standing in adoration before the Lord and Giver of its life; and its response to its surroundings physical and spiritual, in love and pain, fulfillment and sacrifice, in home, work, social contacts, aesthetic and intellectual experience must subserve this, its first duty. All must be brought to the altar and consecrated to the purposes of the Holy. All, directly or overtly, must hallow the Name of God.

 CHARITY

From *The House of the Soul*, Chapter 7

The House of the Soul, published in 1929, concerns the virtues that live on the two floors of the soul's house. The lower story, rooted in our animal nature and oriented toward this world, is "inhabited" by Temperance, Prudence, and Fortitude. The upper story, straining toward heaven, is the home of Faith, Hope, and Charity. We need the virtues of both floors to live truly human lives.

Charity is no easy emotion. It does not merely consist in yielding to the unspeakable attraction of God. We are often terrified and always shamed when we see what its achievement involved for the saints; what steady endurance of darkness, what suffering and courage are the price of their love, joy and peace. The fire of Charity, lit in the soul, needs careful tending. The first tiny flame must not be allowed to die down for lack of fuel; and we may have to feed it with things we should prefer to keep for ourselves. It will only be developed and kept burning in a life informed by prayer—faithful, steady, mortified, self-oblivious prayer, the humble aspiration of the spirit to its Source. Indeed, the very object of prayer is to increase and maintain Charity, the loving friendship of the soul with God.

All other aspects of the inner life are subsidiary to this and only of value insofar as they contribute to it. For the prayer of Charity introduces us into the very atmosphere and presence of God, that secret chamber of the soul where God dwells. It shows us, obscurely but intensely, God as the one object of this soul's love and longing, and all struggles and sacrifices made in God's interests as forms of joy. It lifts the heavy cloud of self-occupation from our spirits, transforms the mental and moral problems that torture us. They all look different in the light of that fire. "Love," says Thomas à Kempis, "sees reasons to fear and does not fear but flames ever upward as a lively torch or sparkle of fire." And it is this constant, desirous aspiration of the soul toward the Beloved Perfection, with its utter forgetfulness of personal dreads and risks, that delivers it from evil.

Within the prayer of Charity, too, we catch a glimpse of our own small life in the light of God, and of our own soul's house as it is meant to be—a habitation of the Creative Love. It is a bracing and a humbling vision. We see our vocation then, however prosaic, as a form of Charity—simply a call to express the creative love infused into us, in this or that way. For Charity introduces the soul into a vast organism, built of all striving, loving spirits, an organism that is destined to be possessed and used by God for creative and redemptive work within the world.

Hence the only active works worth doing or worth having are ultimately found to be those that proceed from Charity. They are the work of a soul adhering to God and acting as God's tool. If the quality of charity is in our work, that work, however

modest, will suffice. If not, all its apparent devoted-
ness, efficiency, and success will merely give out the
correct but unmusical noise of the gong or the tinkle
of the bright and busy cymbal. Works of mercy done
by the saints come out, as it were, almost of themselves, from a soul so utterly merged in the Love of
God that God acts through it. Thus they have an
effect quite out of proportion to their apparent scope.
A real act of Charity is the exact opposite of an act of
philanthropy. It is done wholly to, for, and in God; it
is done for God's sake, as a contribution to God's purpose, because we see the situation from God's point
of view. It is born of the First, not the Second, Com-
mandment: of supernatural, not of natural, love. So,
too, all religious acts and sacrifices—more, all sacred
objects, symbols, and devotions, even to the loftiest
degrees of mental prayer—are only of spiritual worth
if soaked in Charity and used with Charity: with
a loving tendency of the naked will through them
to God.

All the exercises of the devotional life fall under
this law. The use of the crucifix or meditation on
Christ's Life and Passion is found to be of value to
the soul because each conveys love and evokes love,
and so feeds the fire at the heart of personality. The
disciplines and renunciations that give order and
beauty to the soul's house are only fruitful when
undertaken for the sake of Charity. The house is
meant to radiate that; our business is to take away
everything that interferes. This is the principle that
gives all valid asceticism its meaning and worth. So

the spirit of poverty, deliberately loosening its clutch on possessions; the spirit of chastity, calling in all vagrant, immoderate, and distracting desires; and the spirit of obedience, subduing its will to the overruling Divine Will, give health, strength, and order to the love that is intended to find its goal in God. But they only impoverish or sterilize the soul that is seeking for self-fulfillment by these paths. "Charity," says Augustine Baker, "lives and grows according to the measure that self-love is abated, and no further." We have reached the "short point" as the lawyers say, the one thing needful, the all-sufficing rule by which the house is to be run.

Thus in the last resort Christian perfection—in fact the whole course of the spiritual life—is found to be the same thing as Charity: the loving union of the human spirit with the Eternal Spirit of God. Nothing but this Love will drive it to the heroic struggles, self-stripping, and purifications or maintain it through the long, slow climb with many humbling falls whereby it is remade in the image of the Absolute Love. The soul that plays for safety, even spiritual safety, never becomes perfect. "Real Charity," says Saint John of the Cross, "is not shown merely by tender feelings, but by a strength, courage, and endurance unknown to other souls." The true lovers, wholly given to God and God's interests, are released from all carefulness about their own interests, safety, and comfort. Thus not Faith and Hope alone, but Prudence, Temperance, and Fortitude, too, are found in the last resort to be swallowed up in Charity.

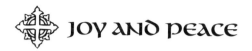 JOY AND PEACE

From *The Fruits of the Spirit*, Chapter 2

The Fruits of the Spirit, *from a series of retreat addresses given in May 1936, was published in 1942, after Underhill's death. She uses the list from Galatians 5:22-23: "The fruit of the Spirit is love, joy, peace, patience, kindness, generosity, faithfulness, gentleness, and self-control." Here she talks about joy and peace.*

Joy and peace come into our lives then, when we mind more about God than we do about ourselves, when we realize what the things that matter really are. The Spirit clears up our problems about what we want or ought to be at, simplifies us and throws us back again and again on the deep and peaceful action of God. Then, whether God speeds us up or slows us down, accepts our notions or sets them aside, gives us what we want or takes it away, gives us a useful job of work or puts us on the shelf, that serenity that is a fruit of the Spirit, a sign of God's secret support, does not fail us.

This, of course, applies very specially to fluctuations in our prayer and that constant struggle with distracting thoughts, that humiliating sense of deadness and incapacity, that always accompany spiritual growth and teach us humility. A peace and joy that depend on how we feel in prayer are not going to last very long. They must be based not on how we are, but on what God is.

Joy's very being is lost in the great tide of selfless delight—creation's response to the infinite loving of God. But, of course, the point for us is that this selfless joy has got to go on at times when we ourselves are in the dark, obsessed by the sorrow of life, so that we feel no joy because we cannot gaze at the beauty. Joy is a fruit of the Spirit, not of our gratified emotions. *Come, bless the Lord, all you servants of the Lord, who stand by night in the house of the Lord! Lift up your hands to the holy place, and bless the Lord.*

There is always a night shift and sooner or later we are put on it. The praise does not cease with the fading of the light, but goes on through the spiritual night as well as the spiritual day. And if you are picked for the night shift—well, praise the Lord. Lift up your hands in the dark sanctuary of your soul when you are tempted to wonder what is the good of it all, and praise the Lord! And *the Lord, maker of heaven and earth, will bless you from Zion.* What is Zion? The hill of the Lord, having at its summit the temple God, the altar of sacrifice and Holy of Holies, our oblation and God's Presence. That is where the blessing comes from; out of Zion shall God appear in perfect Beauty.

When Titus took the temple of Jerusalem he broke into the Holy of Holies desiring to see what the God of the Jews looked like. He came back saying the whole thing was fraudulent, the shrine was empty, there was nothing there. But that was his mistake. There was everything there—for the Holy is nothing that we can see or think or feel. Yet from that apparent emptiness in that apparent darkness, the ceaseless pressure of the Heart of God sends out streams of Love, Joy, and Peace into the world. That is the blessing given us out of Zion: God entering time and space by this narrow door and coming to God's creatures' hearts.

All acts, thoughts, tendencies that oppose the pressure of the spiritual life within us hinder us from bringing forth the Spirit's fruits. So this will include all that diminishes or opposes joy and peace that ought to spread from Christian souls; all deliberate restlessness, fuss, anxiety, all suspiciousness and bitterness, all excursions into the garden to eat either religious or political worms, the delightful luxury of spiritual grousing, those meditations on our own unworthiness and unfortunate temperaments and so on that we sometimes mistake for humility. All these are sins against the Spirit of Joy and Peace.

If we want to be sturdy Christians, strong in spirit, useful to God, all these have got to go. Again, consider how we allow our small, self-interested worries, our self-consciousness, to break our peace— little emotional conflicts, rampant possessiveness and vanity, social or physical disabilities, disappointed egotism, a sense of being slighted, or anxiety about the future. What about the future? Eternity has no future. It is the Peace of God that no one, however powerful, can take away from those who have it; and whoever is born of the Spirit has it now. We see that again and again in the lives of the saints—perhaps nowhere better than in Saint Paul from whom this great list of the fruits of the Spirit comes. Just consider his life and times as the scene in which he brought forth the fruits of joy and peace.

Even putting it quite moderately Saint Paul had at least as much to put up with as most of us— uncertain health, always a bad drag on a public career; a physique not really strong enough for his intrepid and energetic soul; an awkward past to live down and an awkward temperament to live with; right through his Christian life the constant menace of persecution and danger; and finally imprisonment and death. All rather depressing factors in life. Most depressing of all, the failure of his children in Christ, his churches, to live up to his great hopes and ideals. Consider Saint Paul as he is writing the most joyous of his epistles, Philippians. To begin with he is in prison—that born traveler and citizen of the world— never alone and probably chained to a soldier. That cannot have been much fun. We sometimes grouse because we have not enough opportunity of being alone with God. Saint Paul, founder of the Western Church, once he had put on the harness of Christ can hardly ever have been alone with God. And in this same letter to the Philippians he mentions that, except for Timothy, he has no one he can send to them with confidence. "They all seek their own," he says in effect, "and not the things of Jesus Christ." A very bitter admission to have to make for a leader at the end of a great missionary career. But even that does not depress him: *But even if I am being poured out as a libation* (that splendid symbol of a nonutilitarian sacrifice) *over the sacrifice and the offering of your faith, I am glad and rejoice with all of you—and in the same way you also must be glad and rejoice with me.* That is what he cares about—not to have run in vain or labored in vain, but that his sacrifice is available for their faith. In that he rejoices. That, not his great place in history, is our proof of Saint Paul's sanctity. The Fruit of the Spirit is Joy—the rest, he says, counts as "dung"; *Rejoice in the Lord always; again I will say, Rejoice.*

 GOODNESS AND
FAITHFULNESS

*Continuing through Paul's list of the fruits of the Spirit,
Underhill comes to goodness ("generosity" in the NRSV) and
faithfulness.*

Goodness and Faithfulness—we think of them
as the supreme virtues of plain people. Yet they, too,
are the fruits of the Spirit. In the long run we cannot
really manage them without God. The good citizen,
good employer, good artist, good worker—the faithful husband or wife or mother—in these, too, Divine
Love, selfless charity, is bringing forth its fruits
within the natural order and on the natural scale:
proclaiming the dignity and possibilities of our
human life on all levels, disclosing the full meaning of
the Word made flesh. Another lesson in not being
high-minded; another invitation to come off our self-
chosen spiritual perch, whatever it may be, and face
the facts of human life.

Faithfulness is consecration in overalls. It is the
steady acceptance and performance of the common
duty and immediate task without any reference to
personal preferences—because it is there to be done
and so is a manifestation of the Will of God. It is
Elizabeth Leseur settling down each day to do the
household accounts quite perfectly (when she would

much rather have been in church) and saying, "The duties of my station come before everything else." It is Brother Lawrence taking his turn in the kitchen, and Saint Francis de Sales taking the burden of a difficult diocese and saying, "I have now little time for prayer—but I do what is the same."

The fruits of the Spirit get less and less showy as we go on. Faithfulness means continuing quietly with the job we have been given, in the situation where we have been placed; not yielding to the restless desire for change. It means tending the lamp quietly for God without wondering how much longer it has got to go on. Steady, unsensational driving, taking good care of the car. A lot of the road to heaven has to be taken at thirty miles per hour. It means keeping everything in your charge in good order for love's sake, rubbing up the silver, polishing the glass even though you know the Master will not be looking round the pantry next weekend. If your life is really part of the apparatus of the Spirit, that is the sort of life it must be. You have got to be the sort of cat who can be left alone with the canary; the sort of dog who follows, hungry and thirsty but tail up, to the very end of the day.

Faithfulness and Goodness—they *are* doggy qualities. Fancy that as a Fruit of the Spirit! But then the Spirit is Love, and doggy love is a very good sort of love: humble, selfless, and enduring. Faithfulness is the quality of the friend, refusing no test and no trouble, loyal, persevering; not at the mercy of emotional ups and downs or getting tired when things are tiresome. In the interior life of prayer faithfulness points steadily to God and God's purposes, away from self and its preoccupations, especially spiritual preoccupations. It was a very faithful soul who said, "We ought simply to hate thinking of our own spiritual lives." You cannot imagine a nice retriever fussing about his own inner state, carefully inspecting his sins, or worrying about whether he is being directed quite right. He just trusts his master and his own sense of smell and carries on.

The indwelling Spirit of God is never a source of trouble and scruple, but a stabilizing power, a constant. *If I ascend to heaven, you are there; if I make my bed in Sheol, you are there*—when I am exultant and when I am depressed. *Darkness is as light to you.* The friendship of God is like that, and God asks the same faithfulness from us in return. It takes a brave and loving soul to understand and respond to this sturdy faithfulness of God, for there is nothing sentimental about it. *In faithfulness you have humbled me*, says the Psalmist. The faithful father and teacher does what is needed, not what is nice. He will even risk losing the child's affection rather than fail the child's real needs—giving stern tests when tests are needed, withdrawing apparent support that courage and initiative may be learned, giving the distasteful duty, withdrawing the dangerous joy, bit by bit producing in the soul a fidelity that shall answer his or her own.

Surely we may say that the chief struggle of the

Passion, the awful crisis of Gethsemane, was a struggle in which we are shown the supreme heights of faithfulness, a struggle for strength to see it through to the end, whatever the cost. *Remove this cup from me; yet, not my will but yours be done.*

The first step taken towards Calvary was the worst: but in the first step all was achieved. *Be faithful until death, and I will give you the crown of life.* Faithfulness is one of the sturdy qualities most dear to the heart of God. Peter was offered just the same chance of the same royal virtue. Jesus was victorious on the Cross. Peter was defeated, warming himself by the fire, for the night was cold. I wonder how we should act if the same sort of crisis, charged with fear and quite devoid of consolation, came our way? It is a crisis that, in some form, all the saints have had to face.

You remember the noble figure of Faithful in *Pilgrim's Progress*, Christian's best friend. How he started from the City of Destruction some time after Christian but soon passed him on the road because he never thought it necessary to linger, to ask for help or explanations in the House of the Interpreter, or worry about dangers in the way. He just plodded steadily on. Christian, who is the sort of excellent man who gets full value out of all obstacles, worries constantly and leaves nothing to chance; he is surprised to find how well Faithful has got on and says, "But what about the lions in the path?" Faithful said he had never noticed any lions; he thought they must have been having their after-dinner snooze. And when he got to the Valley of Humiliation, he was attacked by two temptations, one to shame and one to discontent, but made short work of both. After that he went all the way in sunshine through the Valley of Humiliation and the terrible Valley of the Shadow of Death.

That, I think, is one of Bunyan's loveliest bits. Faithful is the least self-occupied of all the pilgrims. We hear nothing about his burden or fatigue or difficulty or the poor state of the road. Christian makes a good deal of the Valley of Humiliation, tells us about how horrible it was, and feels it very remarkable that he ever got through the Valley of the Shadow of Death. There is none of that in Faithful. He is not thinking about saving his soul. He is thinking about God. And so he goes in sunshine all the way.

 # POVERTY, CHASTITY, OBEDIENCE

From *The Fruits of the Spirit*, letter for Lent, 1941

The Fruits of the Spirit, *in addition to the retreat
lectures, includes several letters Underhill wrote to a circle of
friends called The Prayer Group or The Theological Kinder-
garten. Originally they met in person to discuss theology
and the spiritual life. But when World War II made such
meetings impractical, Underhill began to write letters
suggesting reading and devotional exercises, usually tied in
with the season of the church year. For Lent of 1940, she
suggested specific spiritual disciplines. A year later, she urged
her friends to move beyond surface actions to the deeper
disciplines of poverty, chastity, and obedience.*

Our Lord demanded great renunciation of
those who wanted to follow him. He never suggested
that the Christian life was an easy or comfortable
affair. The substance of what he asked is summed up
in what are called the "evangelical counsels" —
Poverty, Chastity, and Obedience. We know that
those who enter religious communities accept these
counsels in their most literal form. They do give up
all their possessions, their natural and human relationships, the freedom of their wills. But in one way
or another, something of their spirit is needed by
everyone who really desires to follow Christ. The
New Testament means what it says when it demands

poverty of spirit, purity of heart, and filial obedience from all who would do this. And the reason is that each of these qualities in a different way detaches us from the unreal and self-regarding interests with which (almost without knowing it) we usually fill up our lives. They simplify us, clear the ground for God so that our relation of utter dependence on God stands out as the one reality of our existence.

First, think of *Poverty*. Even outward poverty, a hard and simple life, the dropping for love's sake of the many things we feel we "must have" is a great help in the way of the Spirit. Far more precious is that inward poverty of which it is the sacrament. It frees us from possessions and possessiveness and does away with the clutch of "the I, the Me, and the Mine" upon our souls. We can all strive for this internal grace, this attitude of soul, and it is a very important part of the life of prayer. The Holy Spirit is called the Giver of Gifts and the Father of the Poor but this cherishing action is only really felt by those who acknowledge their own deep poverty—who realize that we have literally nothing of our own, but are totally dependent on God and on that natural world in which God has placed us and which is the sacramental vehicle of God's action. When we grasp this we are ready to receive God's gifts. Some souls are so full of pious furniture and ornaments that there is no room for God. All the correct things have been crammed into the poor little villa, but none of the best quality. They need to pull down the curtains, get rid of the knickknacks, and throw their premises open to the great simplicity of God. Our prayers, too, should be stripped and simplified so that they become a reaching up, a free response to the self-giving of God.

Chastity. The counsel of chastity does not, of course mean giving up marriage but something much more subtle and penetrating. It really means the spirit of poverty applied to our emotional life—all the clutch and feverishness of desire, the "I want" and "I must have" taken away and replaced by absolute single-mindedness, purity of heart. This may involve a deliberate rationing of the time and energy we give to absorbing personal relationships with others—unnecessary meetings, talks, and letters—to special tastes and interests, or worst of all, self-occupied daydreams and broodings about ourselves, cravings for sympathy and interest. We have to be very firm with ourselves about all this, making war on every kind of possessiveness, self-centeredness, and clutch. From all these entanglements Christ's spirit of chaste Love will set us free; for it is a selfless, all-embracing charity—friendship with God, and with all creatures for God's sake. The innocence of eye that can see God in God's creatures belongs to those who love but do not want to possess and so do not adulterate the vision of the Heavenly Beauty by their own self-centered longings. A selfish craving to enjoy God for ourselves can even poison our love of God. It is the wrong kind of devotion—it wants to get as well as to give. So the spirit of chastity must transform and unself all our feelings and desires—even the most sacred, steadying and tranquilizing us, and so placing us wholly at the disposition of God's love.

Obedience. This means the total surrender of our wills, which are the great obstacles to our real self-giving to God. The more we get rid of self-chosen aims, however good, the more supple we are to God's pressure and the nearer we get to the pattern of the Christian life that is summed up in *not my will but yours be done*. Then, not before, we are ready to be used as God's tools and contribute to God's purpose. Since God is the true doer of all that is done, it is always for God to initiate and for us to respond, and this willing response is the essence of obedience. Obedience means more freedom, not less, for it lifts the burden of perpetual choice, and in so doing actually increases our power of effective action by making us the instruments of God's unlimited action. When the whole church is thus obedient to God it will be what it is meant to be, "a fellowship of creative heaven-led souls" with power to fulfill its vocation of transforming the world. There is an obligation laid on each of us to do our best to contribute to this great end, and ready obedience to the human beings among whom God has placed us is a very good way of learning obedience to God.

 # TEMPERANCE

From *The House of the Soul*, Chapter 3

Temperance is one of the "ground floor" virtues in the house of the soul, the balance of the ordinary life.

Temperance, then, is the teacher of that genial humility that is an essential of spiritual health. It makes us realize that the normal and moderate course is the only one we can handle successfully in our own power; that extraordinary practices, penances, spiritual efforts, with their corresponding graces, must never be deliberately sought. Some people appear to think that the "spiritual life" is a peculiar condition mainly supported by cream ices and corrected by powders. But the solid norm of the spiritual life should be like that of the natural life: a matter of porridge, bread and butter, and a cut off the joint. The extremes of joy, discipline, vision, are not in our hands, but in the Hand of God. The demand for temperance of soul, for an acknowledgment of the sacred character of the normal, is based on that fact—the central Christian fact—of the humble entrance of God into our common human life. The supernatural can and does seek and find us, in and through our daily normal experience: the invisible in the visible. There is no need to be peculiar in order to find God. The Magi were taught by the heavens to follow a star and it brought them, not to a paralyzing disclosure of the Transcendent, but to a little boy on his mother's knee.

So, too, we observe how moderate, humble, attuned to the scale of our daily life are all the crucial events of the New Testament. Seen from the outside, none could have guessed their shattering and trans-figuring power. The quiet routine of a childhood and working life in Nazareth; the wandering ministry of teaching and compassion, with the least possible stress laid on supernatural powers; the homely little triumph of Palm Sunday; the pitiful sufferings of an arrest and execution too commonplace to disturb the city's life. Christ never based his claim on strange-ness; it is by what he is, rather than by what he does, that he awes, attracts, amazes.

In spite of its contrasts between the stern and tender, how steadily temperate and central in its emphasis is all his teaching: full of the color and quality of real life free from the merely startling, ever keeping close to our normal experience. Sowing, reaping, bread making, keeping sheep; in these the secrets of the Kingdom are hid. Jesus does not ask his disciples to speculate on the Divine Nature but to consider the lilies. It comes to the same thing and is more suited to our powers. He looks at and studies these simple and natural things with the eyes of sym-pathetic love because for him the supernatural indwells and supports all natural things, not merely abnormal or "religious" things. Therefore each and all of these natural things, made by God and kept by God, can become supernatural revelations of God's Spirit. We feel our Lord's complete understanding of the thing-world in all its richness, beauty, and pathos; his careful, reverent, tender observation of animals, birds, and plants; but also his entire aloofness from its clutch, the deep harmony of his spirit with the very Spirit of Creative Love. No cleavage here between the two levels of human life: the spirit of the upper floor penetrates to every corner and transfuses alike the most sacred and homely activities.

The discourse in the twelfth chapter of Saint Luke is full of this temperate, genial attitude to the natural, in its contrast with that intemperance of soul that alternates between an absolute and inhuman detachment and using the world of things in a childish, grasping way. It is a long, varied lesson in true realism. Consider that wonderful world of life in which you are placed, and observe that its great rhythms of birth, growth, and death—all the things that really matter—are not in your control. That unhurried process will go forward in its stately beauty, little affected by your anxious fuss. Find out, then, where your treasure really is. Don't confuse your meals with your life, and your clothes with your life. Don't lose your head over what perishes. Nearly everything does perish; so face the facts, don't rush after the transient and unreal. Maintain your soul in tranquil dependence on God; don't worry; don't mistake what you possess for what you are. Accumulating things is useless. Both mental and material avarice are merely silly in view of the dread facts of life and death. The simpler your house, the easier it will be to run. The fewer things and the people you "simply must have," the nearer you will be to the ideal of happiness—*as having nothing, and yet possessing everything.* We observe how exquisitely the whole doctrine is kept within the boundaries of our natural experience, how it tends to deepen this given experience rather than escape from it. We are being taught how to run that ground-floor life that we cannot get rid of and must not ignore; yet taught by one in whom the other life shines with unmatched perfection, whose whole personality radiates God.

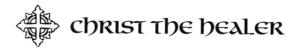

CHRIST THE HEALER

From *Light of Christ*, Chapter 4

In Light of Christ, *a set of retreat addresses from 1932 published in 1944, Underhill pictures a set of six stained glass windows of scenes from the life of Christ, from his birth to his exaltation. Each window lets us look at Christ while it also sheds light on our own lives. The third window shows Christ healing the paralytic as told in Mark 2:1–11.*

Do we think our touch on life—not Life with a capital L, which is a mere abstract, but the actual lives that touch our own, the lives of our own people, our immediate circle—do we think our lives have in them that outflowing, healing compassion? Do those who come into contact with us go away more or less jangled than before? More vigorous or less? More sure of God or less? Are we conveying Christ or the opposite? A stream of vague depression seems to spread from some people like fog from a marsh—that is terrible in a Christian. What *ought* to spread from us is a bit of the Divine healing love giving itself, its power and interest without stint to those who need it, whether on the physical, mental, or spiritual plane.

Now it means an immense self-emptying if we are to take up our part in this spiritual healing ministry of the Body of Christ. Whether given on a great scale to heal the world's disease and sin or on a small scale to the devoted care of an individual soul, it is always a sacrificial job: all-demanding, costly, mortifying self-interest and self-love even in their most subtle and spiritual forms. It has been said that a ceaseless death to self is asked of all light-bearing souls, and this is a hundred times more true of healing souls. We must ignore our pains and preferences, our own longing for sympathy and peace, our times of weakness, anguish, desolation, fatigue; we must go on giving, up to the limit and beyond. Christ himself groaned in spirit at the effort demanded of him. He knew what virtue had gone out; he gave a costly, not an easy restoration to the fallen and weak. He bore our burdens and carried our sorrows.

How do we feel about that? To go where healing love is needed, and give it in a way in which it can be received, often means acting in the teeth of our own interests and preferences, even religious interests and preferences. Christ risked his reputation for holiness by healing on the Sabbath; he touched the unclean and dined with the wrong people; he accepted the love and companionship of a sinner (that most wonderful of all remedies for the wounds of sin). He loved with God's love and so went straight to the point: What can I do to restore my fellow creature and how?

When we replace disinterested healing love by self-interested devotion, when we neglect the needs of the sinful and helpless because they conflict with our religious or moral ideas, when we elude the intimate companionship of Mary Magdalene and the person with leprosy, the nerve-ridden clutch of the possessed and all the variety of psychological wrecks that strew the modern scene in their restless loneliness—then we neglect the interest of God in the interest of our own spiritual comfort. Religious individualists and rigorists should think carefully about this. It is true that God is the unique source of all the healing energies in life. But as God reached out through Christ, so God still reaches out through men and women and often asks us to pay for part of God's treatments. If a tuberculosis patient requires an open window, our contribution may be putting up with the draft. If those from whom Christ cast out devils depended for continuous health on being with Christ, the disciples of Christ had to accept their companionship. One often wonders what those pious fishermen thought about it when Mary Magdalene joined the group. Healing love must drop all personal choices and preferences, all fastidiousness, all desire to get something out of our union with Christ; and be willing to work for nothing, be a faithful servant, not a pet. We may have to see all the resources of Divine Love poured out on a damaged and undeserving Prodigal—the fatted calf, the music and dancing— while we are left in the unemotional and hardworking position of the elder son. Only perfect self-oblivion is going to handle that situation well. *"Son, you are always with me, and all that is mine is yours.* But only if you use it as I use it; come in with me as a partner, pour it out without stint in spendthrift generosity on those who need restoration and healing, not those who *deserve* it."

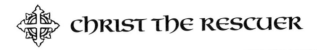# chRist the Rescuer

From *Light of Christ*, Chapter 5

The fourth window in Light of Christ *shows Jesus walking on the stormy sea to bring rescue to the disciples in their boat, a story told in Mark 6:47–51.*

Look at this picture. You see the stormy lake and the little boat with its low freeboard and shallow draft, just as used on the Lake of Galilee now, and the frightened faces of the fishermen. And standing above them the solitary and tranquil figure of Christ ruling the storm; more than that, for through and in that storm he is revealed to them as never before. We never realize that power in full until we, too, are caught and threatened by the violence and hostility of events or the frightful storms of our own unstable natures. It is then that his mysterious action is felt within the circumstances of our lives. *Then he got into the boat with them and the wind ceased. And they were utterly astounded. . . .*

Sometimes we are, as it were, in the middle of the lake and the storm breaks, usually from a quarter we don't expect, and we are doubtful whether the little boat is going to stand it. We feel helpless, making no progress and are inclined to say: "I have gone to bits; I have no help, no support. *This* cannot be a spiritual life." We begin to lose our grip. The boat is very cranky and unstable, the waves very threatening and steep, the sky darkening. We are in utter wretchedness and discouragement.

It was like that when he *got into the boat with them and the wind ceased*. Then the situation was transformed by his presence. One way or another, life brings every awakening Christian soul this experience. When we recognize and reflect on it — for it may come in a way that seems very simple — it fills us with awe and grateful love. God in Christ intervenes between us and the storm that threatens to overwhelm us. His power is brought into action just where our action fails. He comes to the rescue of those caught in the toils of circumstance.

This is a secret that has always been known to men and women of prayer, something we can trust and that acts in proportion to our trust. Sometimes it is on our soul that God lays a tranquilizing touch and stills the storm, sometimes on the hurly-burly of our emotional life, sometimes on events that we think must destroy us or the people and causes we love and yet who are mysteriously modified by the Spirit who indwells and overrules them. We do feel sometimes as if we are left to ourselves to struggle with it all. Jesus is away praying on the mountain or he is asleep in the boat. The waves seem to be getting decidedly higher, the night is very dark, and we don't feel sure about our gear — we begin to lose our nerve for life and no one seems to mind. Certainly life is not made soft for Christians but it is, in the last resort, safe. The universe is safe for souls. The disciples were thoroughly frightened, exhausted, soaked to the skin, but not destroyed. At the critical moment he got into the ship and restored safety, sanity, peace. So, too, when the four thousand were hungry and without resources and the disciples got very worried about it. But they were all fed and fed in an entirely unexpected way. So Christ stands over against history and in its darkest and most dangerous moments we receive a new revelation of his power.

We can never forecast the path God's energy of rescue will take. It is never any use saying to God, "I am getting desperate! Please answer my prayer by the next mail and please send a blank check." God *will* answer but not necessarily like that; more probably God will transform and use the unlikely looking material already in hand—the loaves and the tiny fishes—looking up to Heaven and blessing it and making it do after all. A priest was once asked if many miracles happened at Lourdes. He said, "Yes many; but the greatest are not miracles of healing but the spiritual miracles, the transformation of those who pray desperately for cure of this or that and come back, not physically cured, but filled with peace and joy, surrendered to the Will of God, conformed to the Cross."

He got into the boat and the wind ceased, and there was a dead calm.

So this meditation sheds a tranquil radiance on all our lives. It teaches us in the stress and difficulty of these lives, in conflict with circumstance, in all the tight places to which we are brought in our work, to look for and trust the rescuing and supporting action of God—so seldom exerted in the way we think it must be exerted, yet always present, always intervening in the real interests of the souls God loves. If Christianity sometimes seems hard, it is the hardness of a great enterprise in which we get great support. More and more as we go on with the Christian life we learn the strange power of the Spirit over circumstance, seldom sensationally declared but always present and active—God coming in richness and freedom into every situation, overruling the ceaseless stream of events that make up our earthly existence and, through those events, molding our souls. The radiation of God's love penetrates, modifies, quickens our lives.

COOPERATION WITH GOD

From *The Spiritual Life*, Part 3

In an earlier selection from The Spiritual Life, *Underhill mentioned three aspects of our relation with God according to Cardinal de Bérulle: adoration, adherence, and cooperation. Several early selections dealt with adoration. Later ones spoke of the growing communion with God (Bérulle's "adherence") that brings forth the fruits of the Spirit. The last three selections turn to cooperation, spreading God's love into the world.*

We come now to the last of Bérulle's three ingredients of a spiritual life: Cooperation. What does that mean? It means that we shall not live up to our call as spiritual creatures unless we are willing to pull our weight. The theological axiom that "human will and divine grace rise and fall together" must be translated into practical terms and given practical effect. More is required of those who wake up to reality than the passive adoration of God or intimate communion with God. Those responses, great as they are, do not cover the purpose of our creation. The riches and beauty of the spiritual landscape are not disclosed to us in order that we may sit in the sun parlor, be grateful for the excellent hospitality, and contemplate the glorious view. Some people suppose that the spiritual life mainly consists in doing that.

God provides the spectacle. We gaze with reverent appreciation from our comfortable seats and call this proceeding Worship.

No idea of our situation could be more mistaken than this. Our place is not the auditorium but the stage—or, as the case may be, the field, workshop, study, laboratory—because we ourselves form part of the creative apparatus of God, or at least are meant to form part of the creative apparatus of God. God made us in order to use us, and use us in the most profitable way: for God's purpose, not ours. To live a spiritual life means subordinating all other interests to that single fact. Sometimes our position seems to be that of tools—taken up when wanted, used in ways we had not expected for an object on which our opinion is not asked, and then laid down. Sometimes we are the currency used in some great operation, of which the purpose is not revealed to us. Sometimes we are servants, left year in, year out to the same monotonous job. Sometimes we are conscious fellow workers with the Perfect, striving to bring the Kingdom in. But whatever our particular place or job may be, it means the austere conditions of the workshop, not the freelance activities of the messy but well-meaning amateur; clocking in at the right time and tending the machine in the right way. Sometimes, perhaps, carrying on for years with a machine we do not very well understand and do not enjoy because it needs doing, and no one else is available. Or accepting the situation quite quietly, when a job we felt that we were managing excellently is taken away. Taking responsibility if we are called to it, or just bringing the workers their dinner, cleaning and sharpening the tools. All self-willed choices and obstinacy drained out of what we thought to be our work so that it becomes more and more God's work in us.

I go back to the one perfect summary of our God-ward life and call—the Lord's Prayer. Consider how dynamic and purposive is its character. *Your Will be done—Your Kingdom come!* There is energy, drive, purpose in those words; an intensity of desire for the coming of perfection into life. Not the limp resignation that lies devoutly in the road and waits for the steamroller, but a total concentration on the total interests of God, which must be expressed in action. It is useless to utter fervent petitions for that Kingdom to be established and that Will be done unless we are willing to do something about it ourselves. As we walk through London we know very well that we are not walking through the capital of the Kingdom of Heaven. Yet we might be, if the conviction and action of every Christian in London were set without any conditions or any reluctance toward this end; if there were perfect consistency, whatever it cost—and it is certain that the cost would not be small—between our spiritual ideals and our social and political acts.

We are the agents of the Creative Spirit in this world. Real advance in the spiritual life, then, means accepting this vocation with all it involves. Not merely turning over the pages of an engineering magazine and enjoying the pictures, but putting on overalls and getting on with the job. The real spiritual life must be horizontal as well as vertical; spread more and more as well as aspire more and more. It must be larger, fuller, richer, more generous in its interests than the natural life alone can ever be; it must invade and transform all homely activities and practical things. For it means an offering of life to the God of life, to whom it belongs; a willingness—an eager willingness—to take our small place in the vast operations of God's Spirit instead of trying to run a poky little business on our own.

So now we come back to this ordinary mixed life of every day in which we find ourselves—the life of house and work, subway and airplane, newspaper and movies, radio and television, with its tangle of problems and suggestions and demands—and consider what we are to do about that: how, within its homely limitations, we can cooperate with the Will. It is far easier, though not very easy, to develop and preserve a spiritual outlook on life than it is to make our everyday actions harmonize with that spiritual outlook. That means trying to see things, persons, and choices from the angle of eternity; and dealing with them as part of the material in which the Spirit works. This will be decisive for the way we behave as to our personal, social, and national obligations. It will decide the papers we read, the movements we support, the kind of administrators we vote for, our attitude to social and international justice. For though we may renounce the world for ourselves, refuse the attempt to get anything out of it, we have to accept it as the sphere in which we are to cooperate with the Spirit and try to do the Will. Therefore the prevalent notion that spirituality and politics have nothing to do with one another is the exact opposite of the truth. Once it is accepted in a realistic sense, the Spiritual Life has everything to do with politics. It means that certain convictions about God and the world become the moral and spiritual imperatives of our life; this must be decisive for the way we choose to behave about that bit of the world over which we have been given a limited control.

The life of this planet, and especially its human life, is a life in which something has gone wrong, and badly wrong. Every time that we see an unhappy face, an unhealthy body, hear a bitter or despairing word, we are reminded of that. The occasional dazzling flashes of pure beauty, pure goodness, pure love that show us what God wants and what God is, only throw into more vivid relief the horror of cruelty, greed, oppression, hatred, ugliness; and also the mere muddle and stupidity that frustrate and bring suffering into life. Unless we put on blinkers, we can hardly avoid seeing all this; and unless we are warmly wrapped up in our own cozy ideas and absorbed in our own interests, we surely cannot help feeling the sense of obligation, the shame of acquiescence, the call to do something about it. To say day by day, *Your Kingdom come*—if these tremendous words really stand for a conviction and desire—does not mean "I quite hope that someday the Kingdom of God will be established, and peace and goodwill prevail. But at present I don't see how it is to be managed or what I can do about it." On the contrary, it means, or should mean, "Here am I! Send me!"— active, costly collaboration with the Spirit in whom we believe.

# SAVING THE WORLD

From *The Spiritual Life*, Part 3

Underhill continues the discussion of cooperation with God by lifting up examples of those who have served God with tranquillity, gentleness, and strength. The story of Ornan the Jebusite is told in 1 Chronicles 21.

The church is in the world to save the world. It is a tool of God for that purpose; not a comfortable religious club established in fine historical premises. Every one of its members is required, in one way or another, to cooperate with the Spirit in working for that great end. And much of this work will be done in secret and invisible ways. We are transmitters as well as receivers. Our contemplation and our action, our humble self-opening to God, keeping ourselves sensitive to God's music and light, and our generous self-opening to our fellow creatures, keeping ourselves sensitive to their needs, ought to form one life—mediating between God and God's world, and bringing the saving power of the Eternal into time. We are far from realizing all that human spirits can do for one another on spiritual levels if they will pay the price; how truly and really our souls interpenetrate, and how impossible and unchristian it is to "keep ourselves to ourselves." When Saint Catherine of Siena used to say to the sinners who came to her:

"Have no fear, I will take the burden of your sins," she made a practical promise, which she fulfilled literally and at her own great cost. She could do this because she was totally self-given to the purposes of the Spirit, was possessed by the Divine passion of saving love, and so had taken her place in the great army of rescuing souls.

From time to time it is our privilege to meet these redemptive souls. They are always people, of course, who love God much, and—as Saint Thomas says about Charity—love other people with the same love as that with which they love God; a love that is not satisfied unless it is expressed in sacrifice. When they find someone struggling with temptation or persisting in wrongdoing or being placed in great spiritual danger, they are moved to a passionate and unconditional self-offering on that person's behalf. If the offering is accepted and the prayer is effective, it means much suffering for the redeeming soul; presently it appears that the situation has been changed, the temptation has been mastered, the wrongdoing has ceased. When we find ourselves in the presence of such facts as these we are awed and silenced and our own petty notions of what our spiritual life may be and do are purified and enlarged.

We come down from these heights to consider what this complete self-giving to the Spirit can mean in our own quite ordinary lives. Saint John of the Cross says that every quality or virtue the Spirit really produces in human souls has three distinguishing characters—as it were a threefold trademark—Tranquillity, Gentleness, Strength. All our action—and now we are thinking especially of action—must be peaceful, gentle, and strong. That suggests (doesn't it?) an immense depth and an invulnerable steadiness as the soul's abiding temper, a depth and a steadiness that come from the fact that our small action is now part of the total action of God, whose Spirit, as another saint has said, "works always in tranquillity." Fuss and feverishness, anxiety, intensity, intolerance, instability, pessimism and wobble, and every kind of hurry and worry—these, even on the highest levels, are signs of the self-made and self-acting soul, the spiritual upstart. The saints are never like that. They share the quiet and noble qualities of the great family to which they belong: the family of the Children of God.

If, then, we desire a simple test of the quality of our spiritual life, a consideration of the tranquillity, gentleness, and strength with which we deal with the circumstances of our outward life will serve us better than anything that is based on the loftiness of our religious notions or fervor of our religious feelings. It is a test that can be applied anywhere and at any time. Tranquillity, gentleness, and strength, carrying us through the changes of weather, the ups and downs of the route, the varied surface of the road; the inequalities of family life, emotional and professional disappointments, the sudden intervention of bad fortune or bad health, the rising and falling of our religious temperature. This is the threefold imprint of the Spirit on the souls surrendered to God's great action.

We see that plainly in the saints; in the quiet steadiness of spirit with which they meet the vicissitudes and sufferings of their lives. They know that these small and changing lives, about which we are often so troubled, are part of a great mystery— the life that is related to God and known by God. They know, that is, that they, and all the other souls they love so much, have their abiding place in Eternity; there the meaning of everything they do and bear is understood. So all their action comes from this center; whether it is small or great, heroic or very homely, does not matter to them much. It is a tranquil expression of obedience and devotion. As Ornan the Jebusite turned his threshing floor into an altar, they know how to take up and turn to the purposes of the Spirit the whole of life as it comes to them from God's Hand Saint Bernard and Saint Francis discard all outward possessions, all the grace and beauty of life, and accept poverty and hardship; through their renunciation a greater wealth and a more exquisite beauty is given the world. Saint Catherine of Genoa leaves her ecstasy to get the hospital accounts exactly right; Elizabeth Fry goes to Newgate, Mary Slessor to the jungle, and Elizabeth Leseur accepts a restricted home life, all in the same royal service.

And we see that all these contrasted forms of action are accepted and performed quietly, humbly, and steadily; without reflections about the superior quality of other people's opportunities or the superior attraction of other people's jobs. It is here that we recognize their real character, as various expressions in action of one life, based on one conviction and desire. Thus there is no tendency to snatch another person's work or dodge dull bits of their own, no cheapening sense of hurry or nervous anxiety about success. The action of those whose lives are given to the Spirit has in it something of the leisure of Eternity; because of this, they achieve far more than those whose lives are enslaved by the rush and hurry, the unceasing tick-tick of the world. In the spiritual life it is very important to get our timing right. Otherwise we tend to forget that God, who is greater than our heart, is greater than our job, too. It is only when we have learned all that this means that we possess the key to the Kingdom of Heaven.

fAITH IN
UNCERTAIN TIMES

From *The Fruits of the Spirit*, letter for Eastertide, 1941

This call to vanquish evil by the power of love was Underhill's last letter to the Prayer Group. Her final illness began shortly before Pentecost, when the next one would have been due.

From talks that I have had with some of you lately and letters that I have received, I gather that the keeping of our rule of prayer and especially the sort of life and outlook that ought to go with the prayer does not get easier as time goes on. Most of you are very busy and often too tired or anxious to clear the space that is needed for concentration on God's worship. Practical life presses more and more hardly. Strain is increasing. We are all more and more conscious of the uncertainties of our time. Not everyone can face the results of an air raid with an unshaken belief in the goodness of the universe and the lovingkindness of God. Institutional religion too often seems stiff, disappointing, remote from actuality in contrast to the awful realities of evil, danger, suffering, and death among which we live. Many of you cannot any longer find time for the regular theological reading that was a chief intellectual interest and support, and gave, as it were, a background to your religion.

But all these various obstacles and difficulties are simply part of the circumstances in which God requires us to serve: and we shall deal with them best if we look at them from this point of view. No Christian escapes a taste of the wilderness on the way to the Promised Land; the wilderness confronts this generation in a very harsh and concrete form. Often it may compel us to dwell for a long time in a mental or a devotional desert, where religion seems dry and tasteless and we find very little intellectual or devotional food. This is all part of our training and helps us, in a disagreeable way, to realize our entire dependence on God. We shall learn its lessons best if we make a real effort when things are most difficult to keep a firm hold on "the great centralities of religion" as Baron von Hügel loved to call them—the tremendous facts that lie behind all our practice— and try to realize a little more fully the deep truths they reveal. If we do this faithfully, as and where we can, we shall find that God will secretly feed our souls through these channels. We shall return to the intellectual study of theology or the fuller and more fervent practice of religion, when the time comes for it, with an entirely new understanding of the meaning and unfathomable depths of its great truths.

For God, Christ, the church, the earthly life and death of Jesus, are not academic propositions, but spiritual facts. We do not learn their true meaning by reading books about them or discussing them but by dwelling upon them in a spirit of prayer.

And there is no sphere of work, however hard, monotonous or homely, in which it is impossible ever to do that. The little story of Saint Thomas Aquinas putting away his ink horn and his pen, saying, "I have seen too much, I can write no more!" tells us more about the spiritual fact of religion, that is to say the communion of our souls with the Mystery that surrounds us, than does the whole of his great *Summa Theologica*. A fact is not a notion about reality; it is a living part of the reality in which God has placed us. As we look at it humbly and steadily, it will unfold and disclose to us more and more of the truth it contains.

I am writing to you at the moment in the Christian year when, as it were, we pause and look back on the richest cluster of such spiritual facts ever revealed to us. Paschal Time, to give its old name to the interval between Easter and Ascension, marks the end of the historical manifestation of the Word Incarnate and the beginning of his hidden life within the church. But the quality of that hidden life, in which as members of the Body of Christ we are all required to take part, is the quality that the historic life revealed. From the very beginning the church has been sure that the series of events that were worked out to their inevitable end in Holy Week sum up and express the deepest secrets of the relation of God to people.

That means, of course, that Christianity can never be merely a pleasant or consoling religion. It is a stern business. It is concerned with the salvation through sacrifice and love of a world in which, as we can all see now, evil and cruelty are rampant. Its supreme symbol is the crucifix—the total and loving self-giving of a man to the redeeming purposes of God.

Because we are all the children of God we all have our part to play in God's redemptive plan; and the Church consists of those loving souls who have accepted this obligation, with all that it costs. Its members are all required to live, each in their own way, through the sufferings and self-abandonment of the Cross. This is the only real contribution they can make to the redemption of the world. Christians, like their Master, must be ready to accept the worst that evil and cruelty can do to them, and vanquish it by the power of love.

For if sacrifice, total self-giving to God's mysterious purpose, is what is asked of us, God's answer to that sacrifice is the gift of power. Easter and Pentecost complete the Christian Mystery by showing us first our Lord himself and then his chosen apostles possessed of a new power—the power of the Spirit—that changed every situation in which they were placed. That supernatural power is still the inheritance of every Christian, and our idea of Christianity is distorted and incomplete unless we rely on it. It is this power and only this that can bring in the new Christian society of which we hear so much. We ought to pray for it, expect it, and trust it. And as we do this, we shall gradually become more and more sure of it.

Appendix

Reading Spiritual Classics for Personal and Group Formation

Many Christians today are searching for more spiritual depth, for something more than simply being good church members. That quest may send them to the spiritual practices of New Age movements or of Eastern religions such as Zen Buddhism. Christians, though, have their own long spiritual tradition, a tradition rich with wisdom, variety, and depth.

The great spiritual classics testify to that depth. They do not concern themselves with mystical flights for a spiritual elite. Rather, they contain very practical advice and insights that can support and shape the spiritual growth of any Christian. We can all benefit by sitting at the feet of the masters (both male and female) of Christian spirituality.

Reading spiritual classics is different from most of the reading we do. We have learned to read to master a text and extract information from it. We tend to read quickly, to get through a text. And we summarize as we read, seeking the main point. In reading spiritual classics, though, we allow the text to master and form us. Such formative reading goes more slowly, more reflectively, allowing time for God to speak to us through the text. God's word for us may come as easily from a minor point or even an aside as from the major point.

Formative reading requires that you approach the text in humility. Read as a seeker, not an expert. Don't demand that the text meet your expectations for what an "enlightened" author should write. Humility means accepting the author as another imperfect human, a product of his or her own time and situation. Learn to celebrate what is foundational in an author's writing without being overly disturbed by what is peculiar to the author's life and times. Trust the text as a gift from both God and the author, offered to you for your benefit—to help you grow in Christ.

To read formatively, you must also slow down. Feel free to reread a passage that seems to speak specially to you. Stop from time to time to reflect on what you have been reading. Keep a journal for these reflections. Often the act of writing can itself prompt further, deeper reflection. Keep your notebook open and your pencil in hand as you read. You might not get back to that wonderful insight later. Don't worry that you are not getting through an entire passage— or even the first paragraph! Formative reading is about depth rather than breadth, quality rather than quantity. As you read, seek God's direction for your own life. Timeless truths have their place but may not be what is most important for your own formation here and now.

As you read the passage, you might keep some of these questions running through your mind:

- How is what I'm reading true of my own life? Where does it reflect my own *experience*?

- How does this text challenge me? What new *direction* does it offer me?

- What must I change to put what I am reading into practice? How can I *incarnate* it, let this word become flesh in my life?

You might also devote special attention to sections that upset you. What is the source of the disturbance? Do you want to argue theology? Are you turned off by cultural differences? Or have you been skewered by an insight that would turn your life upside down if you took it seriously? Let your journal be a dialogue with the text.

If you find yourself moving from reading the text to chewing over its implications to praying, that's great! Spiritual reading is really the first step in an ancient way of prayer called *lectio divina* or "divine reading." Reading leads naturally into reflection on what you have read (meditation). As you reflect on what the text might mean for your life, you may well want to ask for God's help in living out any new insights or direction you have perceived (prayer). Sometimes such prayer may lead you further into silently abiding in God's presence (contemplation). And, of course, the process is only really completed when it begins to make a difference in the way we live (incarnation).

As good as it is to read spiritual classics in solitude, it is even better to join with others in a small group for mutual formation or "spiritual direction in common." This is *not* the same as a study group that talks about spiritual classics. A group for mutual formation would have similar goals as for an individual's reading: to allow the text to shine its light on the *experiences* of the group members, to suggest new *directions* for their lives and practical ways of *incarnating* these directions. Such a group might agree to focus on one short passage from a classic at each meeting (even if members have read more). Discussion usually goes much deeper if all the members have already read and reflected on the passage before the meeting and bring their journals.

Such groups need to watch for several potential problems. It is easy to go off on a tangent (especially if it takes the focus off the members' own experience and onto generalities). At such times a group leader might bring the group's attention back to the text: "What does our author say about that?" Or, "How do we experience that in our own lives?" When a group member shares a problem, others may be tempted to try to "fix" it. This is much less helpful than sharing similar experiences and how they were handled (for good or ill). "Sharing" someone else's problems (whether that person is in or out of the group) should be strongly discouraged.

One person could be designated as leader, to be responsible for opening and closing prayers; to be the first to share or respond to the text; and to keep notes during the discussion to highlight recurring themes, challenges, directives, or practical steps. These responsibilities could also be shared among several members of the group or rotated.

For further information about formative reading of spiritual classics, try *A Practical Guide to Spiritual Reading* by Susan Annette Muto. *Shaped by the Word* by Robert Mulholland (Upper Room Books) covers formative reading of the Bible. *Good Things Happen: Experiencing Community in Small Groups* by Dick Westley is an excellent resource on forming small groups of all kinds.